14 SECRETS TO A DONE DISSERTATION

14 SECRETS TO A DONE DISSERTATION:

A Guide To Navigating The Dissertation Process And Finishing In Record Time

by

Dr. Ramon B. Goings

COPYRIGHT

14 SECRETS TO A DONE DISSERTATION

Ramon Goings.© 2021

All rights reserved. No part of this book may be reproduced, stored, or transmitted by any means--whether auditory, graphic, mechanical, or electronic--without written permission of both publisher and author, except in the case of brief excerpts used in critical articles and certain other noncommercial uses permitted by copyright law. Unauthorized reproduction of any part of this work is illegal and is punishable by law.

ISBN: 978-1-7361001-0-3

Because of the dynamic nature of the internet, any web addresses or links contained in this book may have changed since publication and may no longer be valid. The views expressed in this work are solely those of the author and do not necessarily reflect the views of the publisher, and the publisher disclaims any responsibility for them.

Dr. Ramon Goings
Cover Design: Shantia Coleman
ISBN: 978-1-7361001-0-3
Website: www.thedonedissertation.com.

Printed in the United States of America

TABLE OF CONTENTS

Copyright

Introduction i

Chapter 1: Setting the Foundation through Daily and Incremental Writing 1

Chapter 2: The CWS Process for Feedback and Mastering the 80% Rule 8

Chapter 3: Reinvent Your Expectations and Reclaim Your Time 17

Chapter 4: Selecting a Done Dissertation Chair and Committee Members 25

Chapter 5: Avoiding Dissertation Intoxication with Your Accountability and Reality Check Partner 36

Chapter 6: Know the Rules of Engagement and Prepare Your Family for the Defense.. 44

Chapter 7: Preparing for Defense Questions and Leaving the Room 51

Epilogue 59

About the Author 64

INTRODUCTION

First, I would like to thank you for taking the first step on your journey to achieving a done dissertation by reading this book. I want you to know that you have the skills and the will to finish your dissertation. After reading this book, I know you will have heightened confidence and the strategies to not only write your dissertation but develop a done dissertation committee that will be your partner in the process.

The goal of *14 Secrets to a Done Dissertation: A Guide to Navigating the Dissertation Process and Finishing in Record Time* is to teach you the strategies to manage the dissertation process. Often in my conversations with doctoral students, they are concerned with just writing the dissertation; however, they often forget there is a process that goes along with the actual product of the dissertation. Without having a full understanding of the dissertation process, you are at a disadvantage. Given how much money each of you spends per credit at your institution with potentially little progress toward the completion of your dissertation to show for it, I want you to not only finish the dissertation, but finish it in record time! For the purposes of this book, I let you the reader determine what record timing means, as this is very personal. For instance, I know many of you are balancing busy personal and work lives that sometimes impact your timeline to completion. As you read this book, I am sure you will pick up strategies that will help you to cut some of the time you spend being frustrated to being productive and moving the dissertation process forward.

This book is tailored for the busy professional, however, any doctoral student in the process of writing or preparing to write a dissertation can benefit from the strategies shared here. In particular, I created this book to help busy professionals learn how to reclaim their time to write the dissertation. I have found that time is one of the factors that impacts the busy professional from transitioning from the dreaded All But Dissertation (ABD) designation to doctoral degree recipient.

Additionally, since you have put your trust in me to guide you through the dissertation process, I want to let you know what this book is and is not about. This book does not teach you how to become a better academic writer and/or how you should write the dissertation. There are several great books in the market that address this and the writing aspect of the dissertation is very much discipline-specific. However, the goal of this book is to give an insider perspective on how to manage the dissertation process so that you can stop being frustrated by the lack of progress you may have made up until this point. With a focus on the dissertation process, this book is applicable across disciplines. I want you to take a moment and read out loud the following statements:

- I have grown frustrated with the lack of feedback and timeliness of feedback I receive from my chair and/or committee members.

- I am tired of paying for credit hours and having no progress to show for it.

- I never have enough time to write because I am balancing the dissertation with a busy job and family responsibilities.

- I do not want to submit my chapter (or dissertation) because it is not perfect.

Have you ever said or thought of some variation of these statements? If so, this book is for you! Through my work coaching over 50 clients as the owner of the Done Dissertation Coaching Program (www.thedonedissertation.com), I have found that clients seek out my services because of three central reasons: 1) Lack of and timely feedback; 2) A desire for the work to be perfect so they do not submit; and 3) Frustration with paying for tuition and there is no progress in the dissertation to show for it. My goal with this book is to take some of the insights I have learned from my clients and package them into a simple to read format so that you can implement the strategies immediately. However, at this point I am sure you have to be thinking: Why is Ramon so passionate about helping busy professionals through the dissertation process in particular? To address your question, I want to share with you my journey through the dissertation process.

My Journey and Implementation of the Done Dissertation Secrets

As the first person in my immediate family to earn a doctoral degree, I went into my doctoral program misinformed. As a 25-year-old music teacher at the time, I wanted to go into K-12 school administration as a principal and thought that I needed a doctorate to be considered legitimate since I was a young Black man seeking a position where there are few that look like me. Somehow I had developed the thought that once I earned my doctorate I would be taken seriously being such a young professional. As I progressed through my doctoral coursework I knew that I was going to have to write a dissertation, but I had no clue about the actual process.

During my three years of coursework in my urban educational leadership program at a mid-Atlantic historically Black college and university (HBCU), I had a sharp learning curve. In particular, I struggled with my writing. In my first semester in the program, my professor and now mentor wrote on one of my papers, "I am going to stop reading right here. You need to see a writing coach immediately." While we laugh about it now, initially I was taken aback by this remark.

First, during my academic career up to that point, I never had someone say I was an ineffective writer. Second, I had a belief that since I "worked hard" on my paper, that I deserved an excellent grade. Have you experienced these feelings? If so, you can certainly understand my frustration. Moreover, I quickly learned that my professor was looking to push me academically into a scholar who would go on to create new knowledge and my writing had to be improved to communicate with my readers.

Honestly, that comment sparked something in me to improve my writing. Additionally, I was somewhat hard headed and believed that I did not need a coach and could figure things out myself. From that point on I studied academic writing from authors who I admired. By taking the initiative and studying academic writing, each year of coursework I grew as a writer. For example, during my second year in my doctoral program, I read one peer-reviewed journal article per day for the year. During my readings, I not only read for knowledge, but I read to understand how authors communicated ideas. This entailed a lot of time looking up words in the dictionary to build my vocabulary, which I lacked and keeping a word document of phrases and words that I wanted to incorporate into my writing. Along with reading and building my vocabulary, I would then take class assignments to practice my skill set. Over time I got better and better especially when I allowed others to read my work and give feedback. Despite engaging in these writing improvement exercises, I knew very little about the dissertation process. While I felt confident as a writer as I finished coursework (even earning an A in the professor's class who said I needed a writing coach), I was unsure of the process.

When I entered the dissertation process, I was a K-12 special education teacher who transitioned into a higher education staff role. While I was a K-12 teacher I also coached the men's varsity basketball team at my school while providing private music lessons on evenings spent not coaching or grading student assignments. In addition to my professional responsibilities, I was a devoted husband to my wife Renee, of nine years (by the time this book is published). Despite this hectic schedule, I completed the entire dissertation process in one year from September 2014 to October 2015 even though the dissertation was completely written by April 2015 (more on my delay in graduating below). Furthermore, during this time, I also published three peer-reviewed journal articles, had two edited books under contract, and nine peer-reviewed journal articles under review. I know for some of you, you may consider that I have some unique ability that you do not have. However, I want to assure you that if I could navigate the dissertation process with everything that I had going on, then you can too.

Do you want to know how I finished my process

in record time? Continue to read this book. Each of the strategies I am sharing, I have implemented not only during my process, but I have continued to teach it to my Done Dissertation Coaching Program clients as well. For instance, in chapter two I share the conceptualize-write-submit (CWS) process, which was my strategy to constantly keep working and making progress while my dissertation chair was reviewing my work. Using this approach, I completed my dissertation proposal in three months. Additionally, without my accountability and reality check partners (see chapter 4), I would have never completed the dissertation process and would have grown extremely frustrated when the process did not move how I wanted it to as described below.

After I finished writing my dissertation, and my committee approved the document, it had to be approved by a department administrator. At the administrative review, they thought I needed to go back and add some text and then get it professionally edited. However, I was up against a May deadline to defend my dissertation before faculty who were on nine-month contracts left for the summer. Sadly, the document was not approved in time and I had to wait until the following semester to defend my dissertation. My accountability partner got me to finish the document and my reality check partner put things in perspective for me and made me realize the importance of taking advantage of wait times. In all honesty, being able to wait four months to defend the dissertation gave me an advantage as I was then able to begin to write journal articles from my dissertation. I even had a publication come out before I defended and could cite my own work in my dissertation!

I share my story to inspire and let you know that you are not the only doctoral student who is figuring out how to manage the dissertation process while having a busy home and professional life. In this book, I want you to learn how to leverage your busy schedule to carve out the time needed to finish your dissertation. With proper preparation as shared in this book, you can develop effective writing habits, build your dream team dissertation committee, and prepare yourself and your family for the dissertation proposal and final defense.

My hope, as you read this book, is to think about how you can take immediate action with each of the secrets shared. This text is short in page length and written in a conversational tone as I want you to gain insight that you can implement today. Additionally, I do not want you reading this book as a reason you do not get to writing! Procrastinating at this point in the process has severe consequences. First, you will not be able to use Dr. with your name. Second, you are still going to have to pay tuition costs for no progress, so money is lost each minute you do not act. And lastly, the longer you go without any progress the less confident you will feel that you can finish. As I describe in this book, the dissertation is not written in a day, but if you master the 14 secrets shared in this book, you will finish the dissertation process in record time.

Chapter 1

Setting the Foundation through Daily and Incremental Writing

How will I ever write a 100-plus page dissertation, because I'm just too busy?

Does this sound like you? If so, you are not alone. Oftentimes, busy professionals like yourself are managing writing a dissertation, raising a family, and maintaining your busy work schedule. This results in you having to find balance when you are being pulled in competing directions. From my conversations with clients, I find that the dissertation process can become so daunting solely because you think about it as a 100 plus page document. And I think to get past this block, I need for you to begin to think about the dissertation as small five-page papers that you write in shorter writing time blocks.

For some reading this, I know that hearing shorter writing blocks can sound like an oxymoron. It makes sense because as a busy professional you may already feel that you are too busy to dedicate time to writing the dissertation. And for you to feel accomplished, you feel like you need to have large amounts of time to write. As you read this chapter and this book, I want you to change your thinking. The dissertation is not written in large blocks of time, but in small (15-60 minutes) consistent blocks of time. To show you how this approach can work wonders, I want you to meet my former client Lisa.

The Journey of Lisa from Binge to Daily Writing

Lisa is a new high school principal, wife, and parent of two teenagers. Before meeting her she had just been stuck at the dissertation proposal phase for a year. She initially sought out coaching as she continuously had her dissertation chair say her writing was underdeveloped and she needed a lot of work to succeed in her online degree program. During our first coaching session, Lisa discussed her preference to be a binge writer. So, in her experience, the only way that she could write is when she had at least six to eight hours' worth of time. She explained that this approach worked throughout her academic career and she has always had high academic marks. She even discussed how this process led to her earning all A's in her doctoral coursework.

Now in theory, Lisa's approach *could* work. But if you all know the work of a school principal, particularly in these times with COVID-19 and the extreme pressures put on school leaders, you know that those six to eight hours do not exist. This is the case even on the weekends because as a busy professional you are trying to balance everything else along with your work.

Lisa, as you can imagine, could not block off large chunks of time to write her dissertation due to her busy schedule. Additionally, she found that since not having the structure of coursework, the time that she would normally have to herself was being consumed by work and family responsibilities. Lisa's situation placed her in a precarious position where she identified as a binge writer who needed large amounts of time, but the time just did not exist for her. For many dissertators, this conundrum can cause you to stop writing altogether as it can feel that there will never be enough time to complete your dissertation. Thus, I want to share the first done dissertation secret that if implemented will change your mindset and approach to writing your dissertation:

Done Dissertation Secret #1: A done dissertation is written daily as you never have enough time to binge write.

How would daily writing look for a busy professional like me? When Lisa and I had this conversation about writing the dissertation daily, her main objection was that she had too much on her plate and her schedule would not allow for daily writing. She literally argued that she did not even have time to sit down and eat lunch in peace so there was no way for her to find time to write her dissertation. After her explanation I had Lisa pull out her phone and open up the calendar that she used to schedule everything. After looking at her calendar we saw that every day her children had swim practice from 7:30-8:30 pm.

Prior to us working together when she would drop her kids off at swimming lessons she would typically go in and watch. However, she lost an opportunity here as she would not bring her laptop with her! Little did she know that her hour of peace from everyone was right there at her children's swim practice! After our coaching sessions, Lisa took my recommendation and when her children started their lessons, instead of watching them, she began to bring her laptop so that she could spend 30-60 minutes writing the dissertation.

For those of you who do not see how just writing 30 minutes a day could make a difference, let's do the math. Imagine that in 30 minutes you can write 500 words (approximately 1 page). Within a five-day workweek, you would have written five pages of text. In a month you would write approximately 20 pages of text. From my experience, for a social science dissertation, my clients' Chapter 1's are roughly 15-25 pages long. So just writing 30 minutes per day for five days a week could have you with a complete chapter in a month! Now imagine if you could double the time each day spent on writing, you could very easily have a rough draft of the chapter in 2-3 weeks. All it takes is you not waiting for time to write but scheduling the time to write. After our conversations, Lisa started to develop a daily writing habit. She wrote when her children were at swim practice. Now, she seeks out and finds 15 minutes, 30 minutes, 40 minutes, whatever chunks of time she can find throughout her day to write.

Lisa Overcoming the Fear of Writing 30 Pages

While Lisa was balancing her busy work and home responsibilities, and was more consistent with her daily dissertation writing schedule, she started to become discouraged that her dissertation chair had asked her to write a 30-page literature review. Does this sound familiar? Do you feel or get nervous when you start hearing those page counts? For most folks, 30 pages and above starts to get daunting. It feels like an insurmountable task. I just want to let you know that this is certainly not the case. When you experience this feeling, I want you to remember this second done dissertation secret:

> ***Done Dissertation Secret #2: Think about each dissertation chapter as several 3-5 page essays versus one 30+ page chapter.***

Oftentimes, we think about the final product, but I find that when you break the dissertation down into smaller sections, it becomes more manageable. So, for Lisa's literature review, because her study is on the school leadership experiences of African American women, she noticed that there were five themes she needed to cover in her literature review. As a result of her using our principle of breaking down a chapter into small mini-papers, she stated that she would need approximately six pages for each theme to reach at least 30 pages for her chapter.

For Lisa, this became a task that she could accomplish

not only because of thinking about the dissertation as mini-papers, but also, she combined this with her daily writing practices. For instance, each week she would focus on one theme to explore during her daily writing. Each day of the week she devoted enough time to complete one page of text. By implementing this strategy, Lisa was able to finish her literature review in five weeks.

These blocks of time do not need to be large, but again, it needs to be consistent and every day. You do not want to spend weeks between your writing sessions, as it takes too long to get back into the writing rhythm. I recommend writing every day and to write the dissertation in small sections. If you combine daily writing with writing in small increments you will have a foundational component of the magic formula to finish your dissertation in record time.

Now that you have a plan for daily writing and breaking down the dissertation into smaller pieces, let's shift our attention to learning the secret to overcoming perfection and handling feedback.

Chapter 2

The CWS Method for Feedback and Mastering the 80% Rule

Feedback, feedback, feedback! When we screen prospective clients for the Done Dissertation Coaching Program, one of the questions we ask is: Why are you stuck in the dissertation process? The number one response to this question is: I do not receive timely feedback from my dissertation chair.

From my experience coaching individuals in the dissertation process what can become daunting about the process is that you do not get feedback quickly enough. Additionally, because this process is unknown in many ways, I certainly understand you wanting to have some control over what happens, which includes getting timely feedback.

I believe it is important that you get some of the insider information so that you can manage this process and your expectations. In particular, I want you to understand the roles and responsibilities of your dissertation chair (and committee members) outside of serving on your committee so that you can better understand why they potentially may not give you feedback as quickly as you would like.

The Multiple Professional Roles of Faculty

As faculty members, not only do they have a responsibility for you and your dissertation, but they may be managing possibly as low as three to four dissertators and as many as 15 other advisees who may be at the same stage as you. And I know you may be thinking, "Well they are getting paid, so what does this have to do with me?" I just want you to understand the context in which you and your committee members are working. The plain reality is that they have multiple students and they are trying to balance this all with their teaching schedules and other professional responsibilities. Therefore, it is not a matter of them not wanting to give you timely feedback (and we will unpack what timely means shortly), but their workload is possibly impacting their ability to remain consistent. To provide more insight, I want to briefly discuss the three main areas of faculty responsibility: teaching, service, and research.

I will start with teaching, as that is the most self-explanatory. Your dissertation chair is evaluated on the classes that they teach, and this is often dictated by course evaluations. Depending on your institution type (research-intensive or teaching-intensive or some combination) your professor may teach anywhere from zero to five classes per semester. As a result, their time may be stretched due to the time associated with teaching that includes class time and preparation for class.

When I refer to service, I am referring to the fact that your chair and committee members have to serve on department, university, and professional committees. Depending on your committee members' interest, these service obligations could take up a significant portion of their working time. Often committees require time (anywhere from one hour a month to one to two hours per week) to hold sessions and then time outside of committee meetings to conduct the work of the committee. Also, your dissertation chair or committee members might be the editor of a journal or might have a high-ranking position in one of the professional organizations in your discipline. While at many institutions service counts for very little in terms of promotion and tenure, it is still a commitment that can eat at professors' time.

Lastly, there is research. Faculty have a responsibility to be contributing members to their discipline through their research productivity. This productivity includes writing peer-reviewed journal articles, books, book chapters, and edited volumes. The research component becomes very important, particularly if you are at a research-intensive university where the evaluation of faculty weighs heavily on research. Consequently, if your chair and/or committee members are at the assistant professor level (typically indicating they do not have tenure) then they may need to spend a significant portion of their time on research activities.

And again, I know for you as a potentially frustrated dissertator this may seem as though I am making excuses for faculty and their lack of timely feedback. However, this is not the case as I am providing you with a full understanding of the demands placed on faculty members' time. By understanding the demands placed on them, will give you the capacity to learn how to work with your faculty members to get the feedback you want. How do you work with faculty to get the timely feedback you want? First, it is important to understand the Conceptualize-Write-Submit (CWS) method.

The CWS Method

Now let's turn our attention to understanding the CWS method. Let's say for instance you have talked with your advisor and you are working on chapter one of your dissertation. You have done your daily writing and have broken the chapter down into the smaller tasks like we discussed in chapter one of this book. Now you find that chapter one of the dissertation is complete. This is great! This is now the time to submit it to your chair. You should know that it is going to take some time for you to get feedback.

Submitting chapter one should not stop your momentum. While your chair is reviewing your chapter one, now is the time for you to talk with them about conceptualizing chapter two and what that needs to look like. And then from there, once you have conceptualized it, and you've done your outline, go ahead and write chapter two while you're waiting for feedback on chapter one, because what will happen is, if it takes you about a month to finish chapter two, as soon as you finish chapter two and are ready to submit that you should be getting edits and feedback on chapter one. So again, now you have another chapter to your chair and they are sending you one back.

If you continue this see-saw back and forth with your chapters, you can really finish a full proposal, three chapters in three to four months. I have witnessed it happen with a lot of my clients who are diligent about their writing practices and submitting their work, and then working while their chair is giving them feedback. The diagram below provides a sketch of what the process should look like.

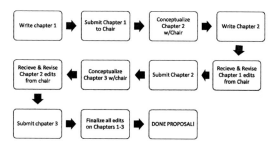

Becoming proficient in the CWS method will allow you master the next done dissertation secret:

> ***Done Dissertation Secret #3: If you want a done dissertation always stay one step ahead of your chair by using the CWS method.***

Now that you have a strategy to manage the dissertation writing, the CWS method, let us now learn from one of my former clients, Carl, and talk about the timeliness of feedback and how that should not be your main concern.

The 80% Rule

Carl, who is a busy higher education professional, mastered the CWS method for his dissertation chapters. But interestingly, he had chapter one completed and was ready to submit it to his chair, but he is fearful of receiving negative feedback and just believes his chapter is not enough, and is somehow inferior. Does this sound like you? Do you have these ideas or thoughts in your mind about your chapter not being enough or being scared of feedback?

Just know and come to grips with the fact that your paper will never be perfect. And this should actually never be your goal as perfection does not exist and academics will always find *something* that could be improved. Oftentimes, many of my clients say that they do not submit their work because it is not perfect enough, and they are concerned about the feedback that they receive. However, at this point in the process, you are still learning, and your dissertation chair is there to help you.

So most certainly you want to submit high-quality work, but just know it will not be perfect. This is why the next secret is related to understanding and mastering the

80% rule:

> ***Done Dissertation Secret #4: Master the 80% rule. Get your work to 80% satisfaction and then send it to your committee for them to push you to reach the other 20%.***

The reason the 80% rule works is that perfection does not exist, and your chair and committee members will always have feedback. Your goal with your work is to get it to 80% satisfaction for yourself, and then let your chair's feedback push it to 100%. Again, the chair's job is to push you to think differently and to provide critical feedback. So, you let your chair be the professional expert who will support and guide you toward your dissertation completion. Do not get stuck thinking that you are not enough. But just know that you have done enough and have gotten to this point in the process. You have completed your coursework. You have probably gone through a comprehensive exam or some other qualifying exam to get to the dissertation phase. So, you have proven yourself worthy. Now is just the time to get through that mental block of thinking that your work is not perfect. You have to get out of your head and not become distracted by fault finding fears. You want to submit your dissertation to your chair so that you can get the feedback you need.

Again, to master the 80% rule, get your work to where you have about 80% satisfaction for yourself, which means your work is high quality. Moreover, a high-quality product is one where you have had multiple people review it and ensure the document is error- free so that your dissertation chair can provide you feedback on your ideas and not grammar and syntax issues. After ensuring your paper is high quality, you can submit it to your chair who will get it to 100%. If you master the 80% rule along with the CWS method, I have no doubt that you can complete the dissertation process.

Chapter 3

Reinvent Your Expectations and Reclaim Your Time

In chapter two I touched briefly on timely feedback in relation to the CWS method. However, for this chapter, I want to talk more in-depth about time. Time becomes very important in the dissertation phase. What I find with my clients, though, is that they often have a love-hate relationship with time in terms of getting feedback. Often the conversations I have with clients goes like this. I will begin by asking the client, "What's your experience like with your chair?" And their reply is, "I just don't get timely feedback." My reply always to that particular concern is, "How do you define timely?" And here is often where I find that at the dissertation phase, students can have unrealistic expectations of time and getting feedback. To illustrate my point, I want to give you two examples from past clients, Tracy and Carl.

Tracy and Carl's Frustration with Time

Tracy is a higher education executive who just completed the entire dissertation proposal totaling approximately 80 pages. Tracy mastered her daily writing tasks and wrote the proposal in two and a half months. Because she mastered the 80% rule, she was feeling excited about submitting her document to her chair. She decided to send her document to her chair and committee on a Friday afternoon at 5:00 pm. In her email to the chair and the committee members, she requested feedback on her proposal by Monday. Additionally, she asked her committee members to get their calendars together to schedule a time for her dissertation proposal defense.

As you read Tracy's scenario you should have come to two realizations. The first realization is that Tracy asked her chair and committee members to respond with critical feedback to her proposal within three days. The second realization is that this type of turnaround is unrealistic. Additionally, I hope as you read the example above that you said some version of, "Well, that's crazy that they would say three days." However, you would be surprised at how many folks believe that three days or even a week is a sufficient amount of time for committee members or their chairs to give feedback. This is a critical stage in the dissertation process and I do not want you to become frustrated. This is usually the point where students sometimes drop out of the dissertation process because they feel like feedback is not timely. Just like you are busy balancing your busy work schedule and your families, so are your professors and committee members. You want to be mindful and respectful of their schedules as you would like for them to do the same as it pertains to your schedule. Although they have a job to do to support you, they are balancing you along with other doctoral students as well.

Another former client, Carl, is a full-time higher education professional. He supervises a staff of 20 while currently writing his dissertation. Carl is used to getting things done promptly because he often is the boss and can dictate deadlines. However, we started working together because Carl grew frustrated that when he submits work to his chair, he does not get feedback from his chair until two months later. I found it rather interesting that his expectation of feedback was that once he submitted his drafts, he would receive feedback within a five-day time frame. With Carl's growing frustrations, I had to have an honest conversation with him and get him to become laser-focused on the things he could control, which was how quickly he got sections of chapters and revisions completed and the quality of his chapters submitted. My work with Carl and Tracy led me to developing this done dissertation secret:

> ***Done Dissertation Secret #5: Your job is to get the document off your desk and to your chair's desk. No need to spend time frustrated on the timeliness of feedback as that is something you cannot control.***

I know it can be frustrating to wait seemingly long periods of time for feedback from your chair. But I want you to keep this in mind, your goal for the dissertation, while you want feedback, is to get the document off your desk to your advisor's desk, email, or wherever it is that they are reviewing your work. I say this because you cannot control how fast they review your work, but you can control how fast and the quality of writing you give to them. I suggest you keep the momentum moving by using the CWS method for every chapter. This will help you to keep moving forward while your advisor is reviewing each chapter. Essentially, you are always a step ahead because while one chapter is with your advisor you have already started working on the next chapter.

Along with my suggestion of implementing the CWS method, I want to concretely address the issue of what constitutes timely feedback. On average, you should expect to wait **<u>four to five weeks</u>** for your chair to give feedback. If you get feedback earlier than that time frame, you should be happy. However, four to five weeks is a reasonable amount of time to expect feedback considering everything that your advisor may have going on with their schedules. Think about the professional commitments and personal responsibilities shared earlier. This is why as long as you stay a step ahead of your chair, you can continue to write while you are waiting for feedback on previous chapters. Along with managing timely feedback you must also be intentional about protecting your time.

Being Selfish and Reclaiming Your Time

In our previous example in this chapter, we talked about Tracy and how she wanted feedback from her committee over the weekend. Here is why Tracy approached her committee in such a way. In addition to being a higher education professional, Tracy is a mom of two. When I first started working with Tracy, she found that because of her position at work, her calendar was being filled with all these obligations that left her no time for the daily dissertation writing. As mentioned in a previous chapter, it is important to write daily.

During one of our sessions, Tracy and I came to an agreement and I said, "Well, since you are so busy, let's figure out a way to incorporate dissertation writing into your work schedule." What we ended up doing, which worked well for her, is that she began to block off one hour per day on her calendar as a working meeting and no one including family could schedule that time with her.

After reclaiming her time and scheduling her writing into her work schedule I noticed a transformation each week in the work she could complete. However, it was another conversation we had that changed my perspective about what it takes to complete a dissertation. As we were walking out of her office Tracy said to me, "You know what, Dr. Goings, I'm realizing the only way I can get this done is I've got to become selfish with my time." That really resonated with me and leads me to the next done dissertation secret:

Done Dissertation Secret #6: For you to finish your dissertation in record time, you have to be a little selfish, and this includes reclaiming your time from work and family.

So, I know many of you have children or are balancing hectic work schedules. You have to figure out ways to reclaim your time. Sometimes, if you cannot do what Tracy did and schedule time within your work schedule, you may have to get up a half-hour early or stay up a half-hour later. There's always a pocket of time where you can find a half-hour to a hour, and that can become your dedicated time to get work done on your dissertation.

As a husband and father, I can certainly understand how being selfish with you time can be hard because as dedicated parents and spouses we are often selfless. However, to get through this process you may need to become selfish will small pockets of time that you can dedicate to your dissertation. To facilitate you finishing your dissertation you should also have a conversation with your spouse/significant other, important family members, and friends who are with you along the process, and just tell them, "At times, I may need to be selfish and take this time for myself."

Before COVID-19, you had the opportunity to leave

your house and go to a coffee shop or to the library. But if you find that you cannot get work done in your home to reclaim your time, you may have to become creative in terms of using space within your home. Are you able to block a room off in your home to write? Are you able to go outside and write? Can you get up earlier in the morning before your significant other and/or children wake up? Do you have a family member that lives within the area that you can go to their house and have some peace? This is critical because to complete a dissertation you do need time to think.

  Now that you have a solid process for writing the dissertation and managing the process, I want to now shift our discussion to people. In particular, the next chapter will discuss the importance of and how to select a done dissertation committee.

Chapter 4

Selecting a Done Dissertation Chair and Committee Members

As a faculty member, a part of the job entails going to academic conferences and presenting research. During these conferences professors also take the time to network with colleagues in the field and mentor graduate students. Because of the work that I do coaching graduate students, oftentimes I end up talking with doctoral students at these conferences and I start talking about the dissertation process. More often than not our conversation turns to the student asking questions about whether they should have a "superstar faculty member" to be their chair.

When I say "superstar," I mean an individual who has a prominent reputation in their field due to their research. Additionally, because of their reputation, superstar faculty members also have developed relationships with key individuals (e.g., college administrators, philanthropic organizations, etc.) in their field. Doctoral students often contemplate having the superstar faculty be their chair because they believe these individuals will give them access to their network which can lead to job opportunities. In other cases, I have heard doctoral students state that this superstar faculty member has research expertise that is directly aligned with theirs, which makes sense.

Interestingly, a lot of times when I double back around the following year at these conferences and I see those students again and I ask them how their dissertation process is going with their superstar advisor, some (not all) say that they still have not received feedback or have to wait two to three months for their feedback. This can be frustrating, and I definitely understand as you may be on a time-sensitive graduate assistantship or are paying for classes out of pocket while working full-time. While true that there are some perks to being mentored by a superstar faculty member, there are some challenges that I will share for you to keep in mind. Below I will give you an example of how this plays out with a past client Mark and a secret to navigating his situation.

Mark and Dr. Superstar

Mark selected Dr. Superstar, who was one of the most well-known scholars in his field. During coursework, Mark noticed that Dr. Superstar was always traveling for speaking engagements and had the teaching assistant teaching most of the classes, or things were being handled online. However, Mark knew that Dr. Superstar could help him get a faculty position, but he just had not received his feedback on his classwork in two months.

Mark's situation is not uncommon as it sounds like many of the students that I coach have faculty members who are very busy or are highly sought out speakers and researchers. However, here is a secret I want you to keep in the back of your mind if you find yourself in this scenario:

Done Dissertation Secret #7: The feedback and timeliness of the feedback you got from your superstar faculty member when you took them for a class are what you should expect when they are your chair, so plan accordingly and choose wisely.

Not every superstar faculty member (or faculty member

more generally) makes for a great dissertation advisor because of how busy they are. This secret is important to consider because your chair is the anchor for everything else that happens with the dissertation process. Oftentimes your work goes through them first before it goes to a committee member, so you want someone who I refer to as having a DONE mindset.

The DONE Mindset

When referring to the DONE mindset, this is an acronym I created that means you want a chair who is:

Determined to hold you accountable

On time with purposeful feedback

Nurturing of your scholarly development

Explains the dissertation process so you always know what is ahead

A chair with a DONE mindset is someone who is on board with you and who you have an alignment with in terms of getting and receiving feedback. For instance, take a moment and think and ask yourself: who were the professors that really gave poignant feedback, and feedback that pushed you to become a better writer? And then also think about those professors who did that along with being timely.

If you had a professor who took two or three months, you did not get all of your grades back until the end of the semester and you never got any feedback, those might not be the best people to have as your chair as they may not have the DONE mindset you need. Again, you want to get through this process and have a done dissertation in record time, and your dissertation advisor and committee members can really slow you up if they're not attentive to you. So again, you always want to stay ahead, as we discussed in chapter two, but you want to consider wisely who your chair is, and just ensuring that they are a person that could give you critical feedback, but also critical feedback in a timely manner.

Building Your Done Dissertation Committee

Now that you have selected your dissertation advisor wisely, I want you to consider the politics of your dissertation committee as you want a committee that will help you get done. Continuing with Mark, he decided that Dr. Superstar would still be an excellent fit as his dissertation chair, so he proceeded to ask Dr. Superstar and Dr. Superstar was elated to be his chair. He tells Mark that he wants him to select a faculty member, Professor Asks Too Much (ATM) to be part of the committee. However, Mark does not care for Professor ATM and he is really adamant about Professor Will Just Pass You (aka Professor Will) to be a member of the committee. Behind the scenes though, Mark does not realize that Professor Will and his chair, Dr. Superstar, do not get along, and they have had drama over the past 10 years before Mark even enrolled in the program.

As graduate students you are typically not privy to the behind-the-scenes departmental drama that occurs, so I want you to keep the next done dissertation secret in mind:

Done Dissertation Secret #8: Ask your advisor for their suggestions about dissertation committee members, and if possible, stick to that list.

They are giving you recommendations of people they have good collegial relationships with, and this will save you time along the way. A lot of times in higher education, you may or may not realize it, depending on how immersed you are with your department, there can be a lot of severed relationships and departmental politics that can impact your dissertation process. You do not want to find out too late that you are in the middle of warring relationships amongst members of your committee. Instead, you want to select committee members who your chair gets along with and who will support your journey. It is important that you consider the roles that you may want for committee members to fill.

Done Dissertation Committee Roles

While following your chair's advice is sound, I do want to provide some suggestions about roles you should have filled when building your dream team committee roster. A committee member could certainly fill several of these roles described below, but if possible, having these roles spread out amongst your committee will put you in the best position to win.

Cheerleader: This committee member should be someone who you have had the most opportunity to build rapport with during your coursework. A cheerleader is someone who will push you to succeed when you begin to feel that the dissertation process will never finish. Their role is to uplift you to keep writing and keep pushing through the process. While it is helpful for this person to be your chair, it is not necessary. However, I certainly understand that for scholars of color and members of other minoritized groups, finding this type of person can be challenging. So if you find yourself in a situation where you do not have access to a person at your institution to be that cheerleader, it can be useful in situations for this person to not even be on your committee but someone you can run your ideas by and get advice from.

Methodologist: From my experience of mentoring doctoral students, the methodology aspect of the study gets the most scrutiny. With this, you need a person on your committee who has some experience with your research methods to provide sound and poignant feedback. Additionally, this person will serve as a buffer and help teach other members of the committee who due to their own research and methodological inexperience may provide suggestions for your work that go against your methodological approach. For instance, this would be a quantitative oriented committee member suggesting to a doctoral student writing a qualitative dissertation to discuss how their findings are generalizable to the population, which is incongruent to the philosophical foundations of qualitative research. I see this person as someone who will stick up for you because they understand your methodological approach (even in cases where they do not conduct your specific method in their own work).

Critical Thinker: Your dissertation will benefit greatly from having someone who is an ideas person on your committee. This critical thinker will push you to engage in deeper analysis. At times their feedback can be overwhelming but you want someone like this to help develop you intellectually. From my experience, the critical thinker committee member is someone to ask before your dissertation defense what types of questions to prepare for, as they may be the one peppering you with questions. Be prepared as this person will ask a lot of questions that could appear as trying to stump you during a defense, but in most cases they mean well and in many ways will prepare you for the types of questions you may get about your work once you defend and are presenting your research in other venues.

University Navigator: The university navigator is one of the most important and often less considered components of your dissertation committee. The University Navigator's job is to help you navigate all of the institutional processes that go into successfully defending your dissertation and getting it approved by your graduate school (or other entity that is the final reviewer of your dissertation). Your university navigator is typically a tenured professor who has developed deep relationships with individuals across campus. This becomes beneficial because if something happens during your process, they can make a call on your behalf to potentially remedy the situation. Think of the university navigator as your institutional strategic partner who will help you avoid the pitfalls around various institutional processes that hinder other students from reaching the graduation stage.

As you read about the roles, I am certain some of you will ask, "How do I even figure folks out to know if any of them can fill these roles?" In this case, I would recommend that you talk to students in your program, take the advice of your dissertation chair, and schedule times to chat with faculty members prior to creating your committee. These meetings can be a time for you to get to know faculty better, understand their mentoring philosophy, and see how they could potentially fill one of these roles on your committee.

Now that you have the structure to build your Done Dissertation Committee, let's talk about the importance of your accountability and reality check partner when the dissertation process does not go according to plan.

Chapter 5

Avoiding Dissertation Intoxication with Your Accountability and Reality Check Partner

As a doctoral student, you engaged in coursework with either cohort members or you managed to create a community with friends in your program. You all navigated the program together, did well in classes, and maybe developed a practice of sharing your papers to get feedback before you turn them in to the professor. I know for many of you reading this now see that the coursework phase of your doctoral journey is the easiest to manage. Your program was very structured and you knew you had courses to check off on your degree completion plan.

In my work with clients, the process changes when you get to the dissertation phase. You are often pushed to work by yourself. This is a reality of the dissertation process because the whole purpose of completing a dissertation and going through the doctoral journey is to become an independent scholar. So most certainly there is some independent work that has to happen. However, when you are in a cohort or you have fostered friendships during your coursework, sometimes it can get lonely, especially when your friends are not doing a topic similar to yours. You may not even have an opportunity to really just talk through your research with them because they may not understand what you do. If you are feeling alone during this process, digest and implement the next done dissertation secret:

> ***Done Dissertation Secret #9: To avoid the loneliness of the dissertation process, you need to have and use your accountability and reality check partners***.

What is an accountability and reality check partner? Keep reading as I share part of my dissertation journey to explain.

My Experience and Need for an Accountability Partner

Your accountability partner is someone you can check in with, someone you can talk to. Whether they are in your program, someone at another institution, someone you may have met at a conference who does similar work, you always just need someone that you can bounce ideas off of.

And just to give you an example, as a doctoral student myself, I established a relationship with my good friend Dr. Larry Walker. During our first course, we decided that we would read each other's work before submitting to the professor. While we both have finished our programs and are now professors that relationship has continued all of these years. If you look at my curriculum vitae, you'll see that Dr. Walker and I still collaborate. This research connection started during our coursework and dissertation journeys.

While we did not participate in a cohort like some of our classmates, we decided to create our own accountability structure. When we got to the dissertation phase, even though we were doing two different types of studies, we continuously sent our dissertation excerpts to each other for review. I would send my drafts to him to get feedback and he would send his to me before we would send them to our committee members.

This really helped us to get through the dissertation process. Dr. Walker and I ended up completing the entire dissertation process in one year because we pushed each other to complete the dissertation. Not only did we push each other through our writing critiques, but we also shared information with each other about how to navigate the process. For example, when there was a deadline for us to make for graduation, a deadline we needed to make for defending our dissertations, and/or a particular form that our committee members needed to fill out, we shared this information with each other.

The key takeaway from my experience is that you need an accountability partner to keep you on task during the dissertation process, so you know you're not doing this alone. Without an accountability partner, the process can certainly be completed, but the journey will be lonely. Having that extra encouragement and uplift is an important aspect of finishing your dissertation in record time.

The Need for a Reality Check Partner to Avoid Dissertation Intoxication

Not only do you need an accountability partner for the dissertation process, but you also need a reality check partner, someone who is not involved in the dissertation process and can keep you grounded and sane during the dissertation process. Here is an example of why having a reality check partner is important.

After a former client, Xavier, defended his dissertation

and we reflected about his process and how it went, I asked him, "How'd you get through?" And he said, "It was rough. You know, it got to a point where I wasn't handling family responsibilities because I was just so immersed in the dissertation."

At one point, his family thought he was on the cusp of mental exhaustion. It got so bad that Xavier's wife pulled him aside and said, "You know what, I need you to take a break because you are just forgetting everything else because you're becoming so consumed with the process."

This is what I call **dissertation intoxication.** Oftentimes when you think about intoxication, you are thinking about being under the influence of something. And this is a case of being under influence of the dissertation. You may wonder what dissertation intoxication looks like. While the symptoms may not all be the same for everyone, there are some similarities.

You are experiencing dissertation intoxication when you are in a space where you are not engaging in sufficient amounts of sleep or you may be drastically decreasing the time spent with family and friends. The dissertation can be very consuming if you let it, but having a reality check partner helps you to avoid dissertation intoxication. This leads me to my next done dissertation secret:

Done Dissertation Secret #10: Take mental health breaks throughout the process to avoid dissertation intoxication.

As a dissertation coach, I find that the chances of dissertation intoxication are typically heightened during the holidays and summers when you visit family and friends. Inevitably, you will be asked the dreaded question, "Hey, when are you going to finish the dissertation?" because your family and friends are invested in your success. But after hearing this statement over and over again, year after year in some cases, the question is typically met with an eye roll or you simply just say, "I'm still working on the document. I'm not exactly sure when I will be done."

You know your family members mean well, but these exchanges about finishing your degree can certainly put a lot of pressure on you. These are some of the moments that build up to dissertation intoxication because you want to make your family proud. For many of you, you might be the first person in your family with a doctorate, and so there is some pressure in some ways because of this title you will have; this too can lead to dissertation intoxication.

And for you all who are writing, the dissertation is

such a large document, it is something that requires so much mental fortitude, that in particular your sleep and mental breaks become important. First, you have to have sufficient amounts of rest. You have heavy cognitive requirements to conceptualize your dissertation, actually write the document, and to navigate the dissertation process. This can take a toll on you physically and mentally if you do not take rest seriously.

Additionally, while rest and sleep are important, it is just as important to schedule social time, time to interact and spend with family and friends. Do not isolate yourself while navigating through this process. My recommendation here is to take a step away from the document at times. I would say if you look at a two-week timeframe, you at least want one to two days off where you do nothing related to the dissertation. This time away helps to prevent writers block and also will allow you to recharge. I am certain from my own experience and the experiences of my clients that you will continue to think about your dissertation during this break. However, I have found that with just a little time away from writing, when you come back to your dissertation after your break, you have a fresh perspective on your work.

I know the goal for many of you is to finish the

dissertation and you want to work on it every day in the hopes to get it done quicker. However, if you go back to earlier chapters in this book and you actually start to implement writing in small chunks of time consistently, you will find that you have plenty of time to engage in this type of self-care and spending time with family and friends. If you are the type that continues to binge write, this can potentially become a problem because the impact of dissertation intoxication can be very strong when you are writing for long periods of time with no or minimal breaks. It will be extremely difficult to maintain this pace with the level and amount of cognitive load required to write the dissertation.

As you think about your process and the dissertation, not only should you have your accountability partner, but you also need your reality check partner. They are the ones that can help you see these signs of dissertation intoxication. I would suggest if you have a friend or a spouse who is not involved in academia, give them this book and in particular let them read this chapter about how they can be supportive of you. So, when they see these signs of you not getting enough rest or you not spending time doing something that's important to you outside of the dissertation, they can step in and be of support.

Chapter 6

Know the Rules of Engagement and Prepare Your Family for the Defense

In the previous chapters, I have provided information about strategies to manage the dissertation writing process. For this chapter, I want to talk about the most anticipated part of the dissertation process—preparing for the dissertation proposal and/or final defense. This is an exciting time as you have done all the writing and now you are getting ready for your proposal or the final defense. And oftentimes I find at this phase in the process, either the program is very clear about what the requirements are or is very loose (and even unclear) about the requirements.

For many dissertators, you spend all of your time focusing on your document, but often do not take a step back to think about how you are actually going to present research clearly and concisely to your committee members and others who may attend the defense. As you progress through your dissertation I want you to contemplate the following: how do I present my material within the allotted timeframe that my university provides for dissertations? This question becomes important and knowing the university guidelines is critical. Below I share insights I learned from my former client Maria about having a firm understanding of the proposal/final defense requirements.

Maria's Defense Preparation

My former client Maria was very diligent and wrote every day and through implementing the CWS method finished the dissertation proposal in three months. As a component of my coaching, I always recommend that my clients conduct a mock defense with me so that I can prepare them for the types of questions that may come up during the defense. I asked Maria to put her slides together for the mock defense.

When she came to me with the slides prepared, I asked, "How long do you have to defend? How much time are they giving you?" Also, "Is there a question-and-answer session (Q&A) after the defense? Who's at the Q&A?" Maria had no answers to the questions. It immediately sent her into a panic as she did not know the particulars about the defense. Based on Maria's experience, here is the next done dissertation secret:

Done Dissertation Secret #11: While your committee is reviewing your document, get concrete information from your chair about the rules for your dissertation defense.

At this stage, you have done the hardest part—the writing. Now you need to know what the rules are and what is expected of you during this oral phase of the process. While there are more questions that you may have, here are a few you should ask to get a feel for the setting and environment in which you will be defending:

- What is the length of the defense?
- Do you get 20 minutes, 30 minutes, an hour?
- What format do you have to give the presentation in?
- Am I presenting via PowerPoint?
- Am I literally reading from my document? What's the mode of my presentation?
- Am I doing it in person, in a room?
- Am I doing it online via Zoom, WebEx, or some

other platform?
- Who is allowed to be present at my defense? Only faculty members on the committee? Is the defense open to other students in my program, to the university, and/or family?
- Do I need to provide food for committee members and guests who attend the defense?

Preparing Your Family for the Defense

Last but not least, once you get all the parameters, you want to prepare your family for the defense. This becomes important especially if no one in your family has been to a dissertation defense before. It becomes interesting at the dissertation defense if your university allows family members to attend. To others not familiar with the process during the question-and- answer session it can appear to be a little hostile because you have committee members who are asking questions, perhaps in a tone that seems very authoritative and/or argumentative. As family members and friends, their instinct is to protect you. A critical part of the process as it relates to family and friends is preparing them specifically for what could possibly happen during your dissertation defense.

Before you defend, it is your responsibility to tell your family what to expect at your defense. You should have a frank conversation and set the expectations for them so that you can focus on the task of defending your work. You could start the conversation by saying, "We're going to have my presentation. There will be no questions or comments during my presentation. After I present my research, there will be some time allotted for questions and answers. During the Q&A, I ask that you not ask any questions."

Let me give you a personal example as to why having this conversation is important. During my dissertation defense, I had a faculty member ask me a question that was definitely critical of my work. When they asked the question, I saw all my family members literally turn around and stare aggressively at this faculty member because he was sitting towards the back of the room. Again, you want to prepare your family and family for this so that they do not become offended on your behalf. I did not think to do this and my experience is a direct result of not having the conversation I am telling you to have. Let your family and friends know that you will be presenting, individuals will be asking questions during a question-and-answer session and that they should just remain neutral because you are going through the process. Most importantly, let them know that this is part of the process and that you will be okay. To avoid an experience such as my own, this leads me to the next done dissertation secret:

Done Dissertation Secret #12: Prepare your family who will attend your defense on what to expect.

Tell them that you will be challenged verbally in a way that they have never seen before and they might feel the need to be protective of you. Ensure them that you are the expert, and everything is okay and there is no need to give evil eyes to the person who asks the question.

Along with preparing your family for the defense, please make sure that your family knows not to ask any questions during the question-and-answer portion. I find that family members think that this is the opportunity for them to be supportive and ask questions. However, they should not because sometimes they can shift the focus of the defense in a different direction, which can unintentionally subject you to more questioning from the committee, especially if your question is one that the committee never considered. When possible, I strongly encourage you to ask them not to ask questions. One, because you are already nervous and have enough anxiety presenting your research in front of your professors, university staff, and possibly other students. Let them know not to ask questions during that time and that if they have a burning question they can hold it until another time when you are not defending in front of your professors. Their questions could be a conversation saved for your graduation party. But just not in front of your committee members! Trust me, this will save you during the defense!

While this chapter focused on preparing your family for the dissertation defense, in the final chapter I provide some insights for you on preparing for the dissertation defense.

Chapter 7

Preparing for the Defense Questions and Leaving the Room

When you get to the dissertation defense you know your research intimately, you have had the opportunity to do a mock defense, and you should be feeling comfortable with your study and communicating what you found. What I am often finding with my clients is that while they feel confident in their proposal or dissertation defense, they are always concerned about what are the questions they will be asked. A lot of times, this brings anxiety because you just do not know what you do not know. In my experience, when I was a doctoral student, during my final dissertation defense, I had a committee member who asked a question and it really just stumped me. While I should have been prepared for it, sometimes it is just difficult to prepare for every question. And it was a question related, not necessarily to my research, but just taking my research and extending it further.

Even now, over five years removed from defending my dissertation, I still remember this experience. I did not like that feeling of not being prepared, so I often coach my clients on what to prepare for. While I want you to remember that you are an expert on your topic and know more about it than most likely anyone else attending your defense remember this next done dissertation secret:

Done Dissertation Secret #13: You are an expert and experts always prepare for their presentations.

A great question to ask is, how do I prepare for the question-and-answer portion of the defense? I want to provide some thoughts and questions for you to consider for both the dissertation proposal defense and the final defense.

Preparing for the Proposal Defense

Your proposal defense questions often revolve around your selection of your theoretical or conceptual framework. Understanding how your study is contributing to the body of literature in your research area and you being able to defend your methodology are critical. You not only need to show why you are using a particular approach and be prepared for questions about the history of your methodology and/or theoretical/conceptual framework. You want to be an expert, not only on your research topic, but your methodology as well.

Some central questions to prepare for are:

- Who are the researchers in your area that have informed your topic?

- What has the past scholarly conversation been about your topic?

- How is your study presenting new ways to inform the conversation moving forward?

The last question, in particular, becomes important because a committee member may ask this question so you can showcase your skill set of knowing the literature. You should know and be well-versed in the research of the authors in your area. You should know them and their body of work and research just like you know your close family members. Remember, you have spent years studying this topic so you should be able to talk about the research with authority and make an argument that you know that researcher A does this work, researcher B does this work, and researcher C uses this approach. However, they have not considered your topic and subject in the nuanced and unique ways that you are presenting in your dissertation research.

Another area of focus is your selection of a methodology. Oftentimes, I see this particularly in qualitative research, folks who just say, "I'm doing phenomenology" and someone may ask you, "Can you talk about the history of phenomenology and the work of Husserl or Heidegger and how this work progressed?" Being well-versed in the research means that you can talk about the history of your methodology because you have studied the historical and foundational elements of the approach. This is also true for quantitative research. You must have a clear understanding of what are the assumptions of those particular statistical analyses to make sure that when you're talking about your data that you have met those assumptions.

Also, at your proposal defense, always be prepared to defend why you are studying your topic. Someone may say, "Well, this type of work has been studied ad nauseam, and why are you continuing this line of research?" You need to have a strong answer for that particular question. That is just something that you will always get throughout your career and not just during the proposal defense. If your study is related to issues of race or racism in any type of setting, be prepared to consistently be challenged. So again, being prepared for these questions, you are the expert, but being prepared will really help you along the way.

Preparing for the Final Defense

When you prepare for the final defense, really focus on how you came to your conclusions. You want to show your committee that you know your data intimately. And in knowing your data I am talking about your data analysis process in addition to your findings. From my experience when engaging in the Q&A after your final defense, remember the last done dissertation secret:

> ***Done Dissertation Secret #14: When you are feeling stumped on a question, always tie your answer back to your data.***

This secret is important as people cannot necessarily challenge you on your data because you are the expert on your chosen topic. The more often you bring your answers back to your data, the more success you will have. The dissertation defense is designed to push you, but always know you have your data that you collected, that you spent time on, that you understand better than anyone else in the world. This, right now, at this moment, is your opportunity to showcase what you know.

Preparing to Leave the Room

Congratulations! When you get to this point in the process you have presented your research study or proposal, defended your work in front of faculty, peers, and family, and now you are done with this stage in the dissertation process. Now that you are finished be prepared to hear some version of this statement from the faculty member who is leading the defense: "Well, thank you so much for your responses. We are going to ask you and all guests to leave the room We're going to have a deliberation about your dissertation."

Many of the clients I have worked with have asked, "Well, what happens in that room once I leave?"

Given this concern I just want to take you behind the scenes in the room for a second and let you know what actually happens in some (not all) circumstances.

Behind the scenes, what is happening is that sometimes there is paperwork associated with your dissertation, and particularly if you have done well, committee members have paperwork to sign off on approving your dissertation. After the paperwork is completed, there is some conversation among committee members. Usually, the chairperson may open the conversation by saying, "We have three options for this dissertation defense. We have a pass, a pass with revisions, or a fail. And how do you all vote?"

Sometimes the committee members are just talking about your handling of the questions and the defense, their thoughts about your actual dissertation document, then they give a rating; usually one of those three mentioned previously. There may be more depending on your program. While much of what is going on in the room is shrouded in secrecy and the unknown, it is not as daunting behind the scenes as you think when you leave the room. It is just an opportunity for the committee to reflect on your work. Oftentimes, what you will find when you have done a really great job is that the committee just has more questions because they were intrigued by your research.

Again, you are doing cutting edge work and your committee members, if you selected the right ones, are looking and rooting for you to succeed. The comments and feedback you received during the defense is just their way of pushing you to think differently about your topic. When you have a good chair with a DONE mindset there should be no setup at this point. As long as you handle yourself as the expert and defend your work you should pass.

While I do not want to scare you, the reality is that if your committee structure is not right, I have seen instances where candidates complete the proposal or final dissertation defense and then committees will ask them to make a number of ridiculous changes that should have been addressed before they even defended the document. One way for you to find out if this might be your experience is to see what they have done in the past with doctoral students.

But again, if you get to this point in the process and you get to where you are outside the door waiting to hear your name, "Dr. _____," it's a great feeling. During this phase of the process, you will have to come to the realization that the dissertation is as much of your work as it is of your committee who helped guide you. So, if the difference between having a DONE dissertation is a few more random additions to the document, bite your tongue and finish the work and earn your credentials! As I often tell my clients, "Just give them what they ask for!"

EPILOGUE

Now that you have completed *14 Secrets to a Done Dissertation: A Guide to Navigating the Dissertation Process and Finishing in Record Time,* you are equipped with the foundational skill set to navigate the dissertation process. As was mentioned throughout this book, the hardest part often is not the writing but managing the actual dissertation completion process. You can be the best writer, but if you do not fully understand the dissertation process you will quickly become frustrated as to why you are not finishing on time.

What I want most for you to take with you as you proceed to complete the dissertation is the belief that you can complete your dissertation journey now that you better understand aspects of the process that are not covered in any course you will take in your doctoral program. Additionally, given your busy schedule, know that if you take the time and truly put your dissertation first (which requires some selfishness), you can most certainly finish your dissertation in record time.

To recap, you have learned the following 14 secrets from this book:

> ***Done Dissertation Secret #1:*** *A done dissertation is written daily as you never have enough time to binge write.*

> ***Done Dissertation Secret #2:*** *Think about each dissertation chapter as several 3-5 page essays versus one 30+ page chapter.*

> ***Done Dissertation Secret #3:*** *If you want a done dissertation, always stay one step ahead of your chair by using the CWS method.*

> ***Done Dissertation Secret #4:*** *Master the 80% rule. Get your work to 80% satisfaction and then send it to your committee for them to push you to reach the other 20%.*

> ***Done Dissertation Secret #5:*** *Your job is to get the document off your desk and to your chair's desk. No need to spend time frustrated on the timeliness of feedback as that is something you cannot control.*

> ***Done Dissertation Secret #6:*** *For you to finish your dissertation in record time, you have to be a little*

selfish, and this includes reclaiming your time from work and family.

Done Dissertation Secret #7: *The feedback and timeliness of the feedback you got from your superstar faculty member when you took them for a class are what you should expect when they are your chair, so plan accordingly and choose wisely.*

Done Dissertation Secret #8: *Ask your advisor for suggestions about dissertation committee members, and if possible, stick to that list.*

Done Dissertation Secret #9: *To avoid the loneliness of the dissertation process, you need to have and use your accountability and reality check partners.*

Done Dissertation Secret #10: *Take mental health breaks throughout the process to avoid dissertation intoxication.*

Done Dissertation Secret #11: *While your committee is reviewing your document, get concrete information from your chair about the rules of engagement for your dissertation defense.*

Done Dissertation Secret #12: *Prepare your family who will attend your defense on what to expect.*

Done Dissertation Secret #13: *You are an expert and experts always prepare for their presentations.*

Done Dissertation Secret #14: *When you are feeling stumped on a question, always tie your answer back to your data.*

Now that you know the secrets to a done dissertation, put them into action! If you have been removed from your doctoral program for a while, reach back out to your dissertation chair or advisor to get reunited. If you are not sure where to start in your process reach out to me and the Done Dissertation Coaching Program (www.thedonedissertation.com). If you are in a position where you feel that your writing is not worthy of review, you need to hit the submit button. If you look at a month and realize that everyone is getting more of your time than you can devote to the dissertation, I want you to reevaluate your calendar and adjust accordingly. Remember, that you do not need a lot of time (30-60 minutes per day can work), but you need to make this time a priority. Since you are now prepared to finish the process you will be able to reclaim this time as soon as you successfully defend your dissertation.

Just know that if my clients who were discussed in this book can finish the dissertation process with their busy schedules, so can you. I am looking forward to seeing you around and hearing about how you are no longer writing your dissertation but now have a DONE dissertation, as there is no dissertation like it!

ABOUT THE AUTHOR

Dr. Ramon Goings is the founder of the Done Dissertation Coaching Program (www.thedonedissertation.com). The Done Dissertation provides individual and group coaching to doctoral students to help them navigate the dissertation process and finish in record time. Along with his entrepreneurial endeavors, Dr. Goings currently serves as Assistant Professor in the Language, Literacy, and Culture interdisciplinary doctoral program at the University of Maryland, Baltimore County. Dr. Goings is the author of over 60 scholarly publications and his research expertise centers on gifted/high-achieving Black male student success in PK-20 settings, diversifying the teacher and school leader workforce, and investigating the contributions of historically Black colleges and universities to education and society. In addition to his scholarship, Dr. Goings has expertise in cultivating the academic writing of doctoral students and early career researchers. His work has been featured in press outlets such as Inside Higher Ed, Diverse Issues in Higher Education, and Education Week. He was named a 2017 Emerging Scholar by Diverse: Issues in Higher Education, and received the 2016 College Board Professional Fellowship.

Prior to working in higher education, Goings was a music education and special education teacher in several urban school districts and was a foster care and youth probation counselor/advocate in New Haven, Connecticut. In 2013 he served as a fellow with the White House Initiative on Educational Excellence for African Americans. He earned his Doctor of Education degree in Urban Educational Leadership from Morgan State University, Master of Science in Human Services from Post University, and Bachelor of Arts in Music Education from Lynchburg College (now University of Lynchburg). For more information about Dr. Goings' research, visit his website www.ramongoings.com.